THE ROYAL OR FACTORY AT HAYES

THE STORY OF A WORLD WAR II GUN AND TANK FACTORY
AT HAYES IN THE LONDON BOROUGH OF HILLINGDON

Nick Holder

with the recollections of Valerie Morris (née Paul), Mary Scully (née Herrick), Ronald Teague, Albert Thurling, Laurie Watts and Maurice Wilby

Oral history interviews by Solomon Yohannes, Jane Jarvis and Nick Holder

Architectural photography by Maggie Cox

Published in October 2011 by Museum of London Archaeology
© Museum of London 2011

A CIP catalogue record for this book is available from the British Library

ISBN 978-1-901992-88-5

Written, designed and photographed by Museum of London Archaeology
Illustrations: Sandra Rowntree, Judit Peresztegi
Editor: Sue Hirst
Reprographics: Andy Chopping
Design and production: Tracy Wellman

The badge worn by Royal Ordnance Factory workers

CONTENTS

The fronts are everywhere. The trenches are dug in the towns and streets. Every village is fortified. Every road is barred. The front line runs through the factories. The workmen are soldiers with different weapons but the same courage.

From Winston Churchill's speech to
the House of Commons, 20 August 1940

THE OUTBREAK OF WAR AND THE NEW ROYAL ORDNANCE FACTORIES

The Prime Minister, Winston Churchill, addressing Parliament in August 1940, spoke of what had been achieved in the year since war had begun and also drew a comparison with the terrible losses and poor planning of World War I. When Britain declared war on Germany in September 1939, there were suddenly a huge number of pressing decisions for the government to make. One of these urgent matters was the need for a strategy to manufacture and supply arms and ammunition to the army, navy and air force. Churchill himself knew the importance of this task – over two decades earlier he had been a government minister with responsibility for munitions supply in World War I. Even with some new construction in the 1930s, there were only nine Royal Ordnance Factories (known as ROFs) in 1939 to supply the whole of Britain's military needs. A wartime plan was rapidly drawn up to convert large numbers of private factories to military use and to build 22 new government-owned Royal Ordnance Factories, with the total rising to over 40 ROFs by 1942.

The production of guns required specialised machines and this meant that the commandeered civilian factories often produced the tanks, gun mountings and carriages, with the more specialised manufacture of the actual guns and explosives carried out by the new ROFs. There were three types of the new ROFs: *engineering* factories to build the weapons and the empty shells, *explosive* factories to develop and manufacture the explosive products and *filling* factories, where the empty shells were filled with explosive and sent off for distribution. ROF Hayes was one of nine new (and one existing) engineering ROFs that were described as 'gun and carriage engineering'

Winston Churchill
at 10 Downing
Street in 1940

factories; the other engineering factories produced shells, small arms, ammunition, cartridge cases and fuses. The engineering factories could often be sited fairly close to population centres, but the more dangerous explosive and filling factories were generally far from London and in more remote locations.

The Royal Ordnance Factories have generally been seen as very successful operations, achieving a very good quality of manufacture combined with some remarkably high output levels, significantly greater than those of the pre-war ordnance factories.

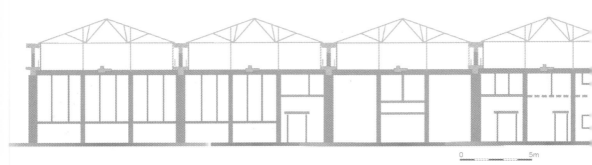

0   5m

THE CONSTRUCTION OF ROF HAYES IN 1940 AND 1941

The proposed site of ROF Hayes was some fields in between the villages of Hayes, Dawley and Sipson (the site now lies in the London Borough of Hillingdon, a little to the north of Heathrow airport). The site was inspected in March 1940 and the construction company Sir Robert McAlpine began work in July. McAlpine built over a hundred separate buildings that year, ranging from small air-raid shelters to huge factory 'hangars' (a map of the site can be found on pages 48–9). The larger buildings were concrete-framed sheds – the reinforced cast concrete beams could be cheaply mass-produced off site and brought in by train. They were lifted into place with cranes and bolted together. The walls could then be filled in with bricks; next steel window frames were slotted in, steel roof trusses were lowered into place by cranes and the roof was covered with corrugated iron sheets laid over asbestos panels. McAlpine slightly over-

A 1951 cross section of machine shed building A

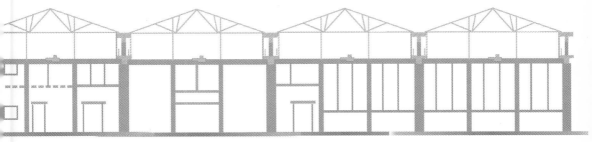

Steel store building W: a few unused concrete frames (temporarily left there in 1940) can just be seen on the left, in the grass in front of the building

The costs of building ROF Hayes in 1940–1

	Budget	Actual expenditure
Land purchase	£22,000	£22,000
Construction costs	£330,000	£311,000
Machinery and equipment	£1,438,000	£1,294,000
'Fitting out' the buildings and other costs	£212,000	£188,000
Total	£2,360,000	£1,815,000

ordered the standard concrete frames: dozens of unused frames – each 26ft (8m) long – were temporarily left by one of the buildings in 1940 and they were still there 60 years later! The smaller buildings were mostly built in brick, with flat concrete roofs designed to resist bomb blast.

Declassified government documents in The National Archives at Kew show that by November 1941 the site was 'virtually complete'. Some 545 'M/Cs' had been delivered and 500 of these 'M/Cs' had been installed: these were presumably the main machine lathes that the workers were going to use. The construction and set-up costs amounted to £1,815,000, a significant sum but much less than the agreed budget of £2,360,000. ROF Hayes illustrates a wider problem in this early stage of the war: the nine new gun factories only cost £3.5 million to build, but they required the purchase of £12 million of machinery, an engineering demand which posed a major supply problem in 1940.

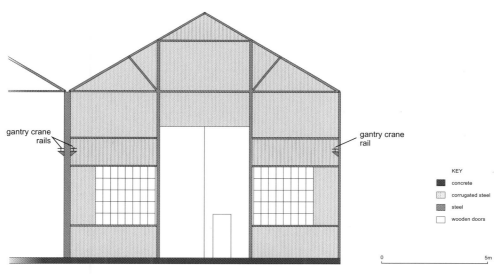

Cross section through steel store building W

The output of our own factories, working as they have never worked before, has poured forth to the troops ... More than two million determined men have rifles and bayonets in their hands tonight ... The whole island bristles against invaders, from the sea or from the air.

From Winston Churchill's speech to
the House of Commons, 20 August 1940

WHAT THE FACTORY MADE

ROF Hayes was one of three factories that originally specialised in small and medium artillery guns. However, the needs of the war effort were continually changing and so the ROFs had to respond to evolving demands for bigger weapons and for weapons designed for offensive rather than defensive warfare. Production probably began at ROF Hayes in late 1941, and the factory produced small 2-pounder tank guns, as well as large 25-pounder field guns. In 1942 production began changing over to the larger 6-pounder tank and anti-tank guns. Later in the war ROF Hayes upgraded American Sherman tanks with larger guns (see below, 'ROF Hayes and the Battle of Normandy').

Other examples of innovative armaments produced at ROF Hayes include smoke shells (which were designed to camouflage troop movement, confuse the enemy or mark targets) and mounts for a new Polsten 20mm anti-aircraft cannon.

Winston Churchill inspects a Cromwell tank equipped with a 75mm gun (31 March 1944)

Three workers put the finishing touches to a 25-pounder at another ROF

The nomenclature of artillery weapons can be somewhat confusing. The name of an artillery gun often refers to the approximate weight of the shell it could fire (hence a 2-pounder gun) or to the diameter of the gun barrel, which could be in imperial or metric measurements (for example a 4.2in mortar or a 95mm howitzer). There is often a model number, usually referring to a developmental sequence of Mark I, Mark II, etc, as the design of the gun was refined over time (and often abbreviated to Mk I, Mk II). The gun itself could be mounted on a tank (hence 'tank gun'), or simply mounted on wheels as a mobile field gun. Whereas a typical field or tank gun fired a shell on a low trajectory over a long distance, a howitzer fired on a high and plunging trajectory over a shorter distance in order, for example, to fire over a hill or down into trenches.

Matilda tank with a 10-pounder gun on exercise in Sussex on 4 March 1941

A Churchill tank with a 6-pounder gun on exercise in Suffolk on 14 April 1943

Armaments produced at ROF Hayes

Armament type	Peak monthly production	Approximate dates
2-pounder Mk X tank guns	165	1941–2
25-pounder Mk II field guns (on Mk I carriage)	110	1941–5
95mm quick firing Mk I tank howitzers	200	1941–4
6-pounder 7-hundredweight quick firing Mks II and IV anti-tank guns	90	1942–3
6-pounder quick firing Mks III and V tank guns	77	1942–5
95mm quick firing Mk II infantry howitzers	160	1943–4
75mm quick firing Mks V and Va tank guns	150	1943–5
77mm quick firing Mk II tank guns (originally known as Vickers HV 75mm)	50	1944–5
Sherman Firefly tank conversions (fitting 17-pounder guns)		1944–5
Polsten 20mm anti-aircraft cannon 'triple' mountings		1944–5
Smoke shell bases		
Tail adaptors and rings for 4.2in mortars		

This is an engineers' war. We are fully and personally aware of that fact ... It is a machine war with a vengeance. Whether it is in the anti-aircraft defences, or the machines on land and sea, or in the sky, it is the engineer who stands behind them all.

Jack Tanner, President of the Amalgamated Engineering Union at the annual conference in July 1940

HOW THE
FACTORY WORKED

The factory's own railway siding brought materials into building W, the steel pool, or building V, the central stores (see the map on pages 48–9). Both buildings had wide 'barn doors' that swung open to let the goods carriages directly into the building. Separate sidings led into the two main machine sheds, buildings A and Y. These two buildings were simply enormous: each measured 160 x 82m inside (524 x 269ft), with the maximum height being 9m or 29ft; being divided by open concrete arcades into eight long aisles, they resembled industrial cathedrals. The factory used standard metal engineering machine tools for the essential processes used to make the various types of gun barrel. These machines were arranged in an assembly line in each shed, enabling the workers to perform the various engineering tasks in sequence – turning (to form the basic barrel), drilling, reaming (slightly enlarging the drilled hole to the correct bore), rifling (cutting the spiral grooves in the barrel), polishing, followed by the assembly of the whole gun.

One of the huge machine sheds – building A – at ROF Hayes

The inside of the large machine shed building Y

The gun barrels and other ordnance products were carried along from stage to stage by huge overhead gantry cranes, each gliding along the eight long aisles that formed each shed. Mary Scully recalled the role of her mother, Mrs Herrick, in the factory:

> *She was the first woman crane driver and she had a crane very high up in the building – they used to put slings up and she had to lower the crane down to move the big gun turrets about. That's what her job was – to move these big parts about in this crane up above us.*

A still photograph from the 1942 film *Work party*, showing Mrs Herrick, the gantry crane foreman, suspended in an operator's cage as she moves along the aisle carrying a large gun barrel

A pile of 25-pounder field gun barrels ready for rifling, in another ROF

Mary Scully herself (then Mary Herrick) was a lathe operator and she described her working life in the machine shed:

Mary Scully (then Mary Herrick) at work at ROF Hayes in 1942

I used to work on a big centre lathe – it was massive – to make parts for the guns, small parts and bigger. This was parts to go on a gun turret. We had a lathe centre and they used to teach us how to do it: we had micrometers [to get] the precise size and they used to teach us. We didn't have a lot of training – two weeks I suppose. We didn't know where [the parts] went and things – they never told us – we just measured them and an inspector would come round.

The finished gun barrels and assembled guns could then be reloaded onto goods carriages and shunted out of the shed onto the sidings, ready to be transferred to the main line that ran past the factory. Albert Thurling, a Co-op delivery boy who was often bringing food into the factory, recalls the trains:

At that time they had a siding where trains would come in from the main line ... and things that they had manufactured were put onto the train and then taken away, covered up with tarpaulin. So once they left the factory premises you didn't really see what exactly was on there because it was camouflaged.

The factory offices were situated near the main entrance, in the south-east corner. The factory also had its own boiler house for its power supply, water tanks, sheds for compressed air plant, an oil store, garages, as well as several other storage huts (see below, for the factory's defences and air-raid shelters).

Members of the Soviet trade union mission to England
inspect a nearly completed 6-pounder gun at ROF Hayes

We in the services owe [the factory workers] a great debt of gratitude for the manner in which they triumphed over all sorts of difficulties and provided us with the necessary arms and ammunition: where, and when, and how, they were wanted.

From speech by Field Marshall Montgomery,
20 December 1946

WOMEN AND MEN AT ROF HAYES

It had originally been envisaged that ROF Hayes would employ up to 2800 workers but in January 1943 the workforce reached its peak of 2442, gradually reducing to 1672 by May 1944. Wartime documents chart the challenges posed by this massive recruitment programme of unskilled staff, few of whom had any engineering experience. For example, in pre-war factories, it took 30 individual operations by skilled factory workers to produce a 3.7in gun barrel; at the start of the war this process was adapted by simplifying the tasks – and increasing their number – so that less skilled workers could produce the same barrel to the same standard. The supervisors and factory managers at Hayes were generally brought in from longer-established factories, particularly Woolwich Arsenal. Valerie Morris remembers that her father Harry Paul grew up in Woolwich and worked at the arsenal before the war; he was then transferred to ROF Hayes to work as a foreman.

A still photograph from the 1942 film *Work party*, showing workers in one of the two machine sheds

Women workers poster

There are no surviving staff lists from ROF Hayes, but a relatively large proportion of the workers were women: approximately 55% of the overall workforce of the ROFs were women, although the proportions of women at the engineering ROFs tended to be slightly lower. Mary Scully remembers the different types of work done by men and women:

> *There were more women than men. There were men who done [some] jobs; the men done jobs women couldn't do: men inspectors [who] set machines and things like that.*

Mary Scully gives a vivid description of her working conditions at the factory:

> *We used to work from seven in the morning to seven at night and we'd do shift work so the machines were working practically continually all the time. We used to clock in quarter of an hour before so [you'd] get overalls on. You had to wear a hat with a snood on the back so hair didn't get caught in the machine. We'd clock in and have a chat before we started work. You didn't move, you stayed at the machine and popped back to work again [after breaks]. In them days, you just done it – it was the war effort. It was a noisy place and it was greasy [from] machines – and overalls go greasy – but [I] didn't take any notice, it was a job and you done it. [We] washed, changed and*

A wartime photograph taken at ROF Hayes; the original caption is 'Miss Kathleen Akies, formerly a shop assistant, chambering 6-pounder gun barrels'

[went] home. We'd get an hour for lunch. It was tiring, I suppose. You were constantly watching the things go around all time and measuring – it was quite heavy lifting – [you] had to stand on a wooden platform. And operate the machine, it was so big.

ROF Hayes was one of a number of ordnance factories analysed in a 1942–3 study of safety and work-related accidents. The factory had a relatively low accident rate, significantly lower than an explosive factory (ROF Irvine), and lower than the larger engineering factory at ROF Nottingham. There were, however, a number of non-fatal work accidents. Three outstanding workers at ROF Hayes received the British Empire Medal for their services: Mrs Parsons, T B Richards and A Sanderson.

In January 1942 the factory received some unusual visitors. An official trade union delegation from the Soviet Union had arrived in Britain in December, headed by the Politburo member Nikolai Shvernik. They spent six weeks touring the country, visiting a number of factories and holding several meetings with British trade unionists.

Woman worker at ROF Hayes operating a lathe, watched by members of the Soviet trade union mission (including Politburo member Nikolai Shvernik) to England in January 1942

LOOKING AFTER THE WORKERS

In 1940 Churchill appointed the trade union leader Ernest Bevin as Minister for Labour. While it would be an exaggeration to say that the war ushered in a period of complete industrial harmony, it is certainly the case that Bevin brought about significant improvements in wages and welfare conditions in Britain's factories. Staffing practices also evolved, generally as a result of agreements made by the union-employer Joint Works Production Committees. The system of 10- or 12-hour shifts often became less rigid, with shorter working hours, as it was found that commuting distances, the need for meals at the beginning and end of shifts, and the domestic commitments of women workers meant that the longer peacetime shift pattern was not practical. On the other hand, the testimony of numerous wartime workers proves that these theoretical hours of work were often exceeded!

The outside of the canteen block

The inside of the main canteen

In many factories, particularly in the early days of the war, workers had been expected to bring their own sandwiches to eat at dinner time. However, given the lack of time to do much shopping (let alone the problems of rationing), it quickly became apparent that it was more efficient to give the workers a good hot meal. The 2000 or more workers at ROF Hayes had their own canteen block and it appears to have been planned from the beginning of the factory. A large brick building housed the main canteen hall, with several air-raid shelters along one side and a kitchen block on the other. A smaller room with separate kitchens was probably the managers' dining room in an adjacent block.

Albert Thurling was the errand boy for the Co-op shop in Coldharbour Lane in 1944 and he recalls cycling to ROF Hayes at least once a week on his big delivery tricycle, delivering a variety of rationed goods to the canteen:

> [I used to deliver] stuff that was rationed: tea, sugar, margarine, cheese, sometimes
> eggs (but not very often). Occasionally on a Thursday when we used to get the
> use temporarily of a van we would deliver on behalf of one of the other [Co-op]

departments – greengrocery – sacks of potatoes. They were a hundredweight and quite heavy to take on a bike or a trike! Meat they got from the meat department [of the Co-op] ... One of the cooks or one of the senior people in the canteen would take the goods from me and sign my little book.

The factory canteen was also used as the social and entertainments block. During the war the popular radio programme *Workers' playtime* was a regular outside broadcast on the BBC, going out live three times a week from a factory canteen 'somewhere in Britain'. On at least two occasions ROF Hayes was that secret canteen, as Mary Scully recalls:

We had Vera Lynn there. She came up the factory, she had her rollers in her hair – there was nothing posh about her – and then in dinner hour she sang on stage. Then we had Flanagan and Allen. We had a square [dance], cleared the tables and we had music and had a dance round the floor, and then when the siren went we went back to work. They were entertaining workers to give them morale, to cheer them up; that was what they called Workers' *playtime.*

View of Coldharbour Lane in Hayes in the 1940s: the Co-op is the white building at the end of the street (centre right)

With large numbers of women workers, ROF Hayes, like so many other factories, faced new challenges such as the provision of childcare. A large proportion of the country's wartime female workforce were in fact women in their 30s and 40s who faced conflicting demands of childcare and running a home on the one hand, and the need to earn money and do one's duty on the other. Albert Thurling also used to deliver food to the adjacent nursery that looked after many of the ROF women's children:

There was a day nursery as you went down to the ordnance factory, on the corner was a big house that had been converted ... The people [from ROF Hayes] would bring their children and leave them, and then pick them up on the way home. [It was] on the corner of Bourne Avenue and Dawley Road ... There was an awful lot of children there! Different age groups were separated into different [rooms].

The factory had other welfare facilities including a medical surgery, changing rooms and a bike shed.

Vera Lynn entertains the workers in the canteen of another English factory during the war

Ladies and gentlemen,

Workers' playtime!

The opening words of the BBC wartime
radio show

File

LIST OF FALL OF H.E. BOMBS - AIR RAID

22.37 HOURS ON THE 5TH INST:

1 Meadow south of junction West End Lane - High St. Harlington

1 Entrance Haywards Farm (demolishing part of building)

1 North of Haywards Farm on G.I. Fence.

2 Cabbage field 200 yards north Cranford Park Lane

2 Orchard 50 yards north Cranford Park Lane

2 Phelps Field 400 yards north Cranford Park Lane

1 Haywards field 500 yards north Cranford Park Lane

2 Cranford Park 300 yards south west Cranford Park School

1 Hit north end of Cranford Park School causing 7 serious
   casualties (2 since died), plus 4 slight casualties.

1 About 200 yards south Mildred Avenue.

1 Incendiary Bomb at 22.37 hours set fire to roof of No. 7
   Roseville Avenue.

   About 20 Incendiary Bombs near junction Water Splash Lane and
   North Hyde Road.

   02.25 Hours 6th instant.

6 West side of enclosure R.O.F. Bourne Avenue.

1 - 50 yards south - ditto -

   TOTAL 21 H.E. Bombs - 19 of which fell in open spaces.

About 50 Incendiary bombs north of Cranford Park and gardens
   adjoining.

The 'Hayes and Harlington ARP incident file' showing the report on
the bombs that landed by ROF Hayes ('R.O.F. Bourne Avenue') on
the night of 5 September 1940

DEFENDING THE FACTORY

The factory at Hayes was a secret and secure site, guarded 24 hours a day by armed military police. It was completely surrounded by a triple perimeter fence, probably a combination of barbed wire and chain-link. The site and its immediate vicinity had four hexagonal concrete pillboxes (known as type 22 pillboxes), which allowed observation and – in the event of enemy attack – defensive rifle and light machine gun fire. One of these, situated near where the railway line entered the factory, was twice the normal height and must have primarily been a firewatcher's observation post. The site had three other single-storey one-man observation posts with narrow horizontal slits. The main entrance into the site was from Bourne Avenue to the east: here there was a gate guarded by a police building on each side. Mary Scully recalls having to show her pass as she came into the site each day:

> *You couldn't get in or out without a pass. You couldn't get into the factory unless you had a pass: there was police on the gates, all security.*

An unusual tall pillbox at ROF Hayes, probably a firewatcher's observation post

The main entrance to ROF Hayes – note the horizontal observation slit on the security building to the right

However, Albert Thurling, the Co-op's delivery boy, remembers a somewhat slacker approach to security:

> *One of the things that surprised me was that I wasn't challenged. I mean the bike and the trike that I used to deliver the goods on was well marked up with Co-op signs all over it ... All this [was] top secret and yet I'm going in and out there and nobody is challenging me!*

There were a large number of air-raid shelters around the factory. Several buildings including the main machine sheds had small brick shelters with concrete roofs, generally positioned right next to the building but not actually touching. The administration block in the south of the site had a strong central corridor with a concrete roof, and the corridor doors were offset from the exterior windows as a precaution against blast. There were a further 11 brick shelters of an almost identical design. Each was a concrete-roofed rectangle with offset entrance lobbies at each end (with a door and a barred window), designed for 50 people. Alice Wilby, an overhead crane operator at ROF Hayes, vividly remembered having to slide down a rope from her gantry crane when the air-raid siren sounded; she hated it because she used to burn her hands!

The EMI factory a short distance away was bombed during the war with the loss of 23 lives but, fortunately, there were no direct hits at ROF Hayes. The 'Hayes and Harlington ARP incident file' (above, page 30) records six high explosive bombs landing on the field to the west of ROF Hayes at 2:25am on the night of the 5 September 1940, with a single bomb landing 50 yards further south. Other bombs from that raid caused four deaths. Laurie Watts remembers going to the field, as a boy, the day after the bombs landed in order to look for souvenirs, and he notes that one of the bomb craters was not filled in until the 1970s.

One of the air-raid shelters

A sign on the inside of one of the air-raid shelters

Every one you can produce will help materially to shorten the war.

Memo of 24 May 1944 discussing the new Firefly tank and the future Operation Overlord

ROF HAYES AND THE BATTLE OF NORMANDY

As the war progressed, there was an increasing need for heavier armaments, particularly for Allied tanks that were coming up against the bigger German tanks. For example, in North Africa in 1942 the British tanks with their 2-pounders had been outgunned by Rommel's Panzer divisions. By 1943 the goal of fitting a 17-pounder tank gun on the American Sherman tank was being pursued unofficially by a number of British military officers. At the same time, there had been several problems and mistakes with the official project to design a British tank with a 17-pounder: the A30 Challenger. The breakthrough came when the Vickers engineer W Kilbourn came up with an ingenious new design to fit the rather large 17-pounder gun mechanism into the relatively small space of the Sherman, in particular creating a new gun mount with a system of cylinders to absorb the massive recoil caused when the big gun fired. Crucially, Claude Gibb, soon to be head of the Tank Board in the Ministry of Supply, backed Kilbourn, and the design could move from prototype to production line.

In late 1943 ROF Hayes (with at least three other factories including its larger 'parent' factory, ROF Nottingham) was asked to produce the new gun and upgrade the Shermans. The principal job was to strip out the old gun barrels and mechanisms, and install the 17-pounders and their new gun mechanisms. The job also involved removing the Sherman's old machine gun, fitting a new armoured radio box on the rear of the turret and creating some extra storage for the larger ammunition. The new tank was officially known as the Sherman IC or VC (with the Roman numerals 'I' and 'V' indicating the original model and the letter 'C' indicating the conversion) but was soon called the

Firefly by the tank regiments themselves. Ronald Teague remembers visiting ROF Hayes in the summer of 1944, when his father Frank was working there:

> *I was in the army, in the Royal Armoured Corps, which was tanks, and my father said he could get me a visit [to ROF Hayes] to see the working of the tank conversion. I went up there and spent half a day up there watching them doing the conversion of the 75[mm] tank to the 17-pounder. [It was] like a big aircraft hangar and they used to drive the tanks in on trains ... they used to unload and then drive them in to do the work on them ... [There were] quite a few women there working and they used to do mainly the work stripping out the tank turret, the heavy work the men used to do, but they used to do stripping out the small stuff ... It was all manual work stripping out the great big things.*

In 1944–5 about 2000 of the new Sherman Fireflies were made. There are no exact figures for the number coming from ROF Hayes, but its production probably accounted for a little under a quarter. These tanks left ROF Hayes by train, travelling to the south coast for the sea journey to Normandy. The Battle of Normandy was undoubtedly one of the key battles of World War II. Beginning with the D-Day landings of 6 June 1944, and the initial operations to establish a temporary harbour and supply bases, it continued in June, with the operations to take the port of Cherbourg, and in July, with the struggle to take the important city of Caen. After six weeks of fighting the Allies broke out of the Normandy beachhead, taking Paris on 25 August. Each Allied four-tank troop had been assigned one of the upgraded Shermans, later increasing to two per troop. The gamble taken in 1943 to concentrate on the Sherman conversions rather than the new Challenger had paid off: the Firefly with its upgraded weapon system was very successful in the Battle of Normandy, as they were the only Allied tank capable of matching and, indeed, beating the firepower of the well-armed German Panther and Tiger tanks, large numbers of which had been hastily moved to Normandy after D-Day.

A Sherman Firefly coming ashore on Sword Beach on 7 June 1944, photographed by Sergeant Laing (top); Centaur IV tank with 95mm howitzer in Normandy, 13 June 1944 (bottom)

A few months after Ronald Teague's visit to ROF Hayes in the summer of 1944, he was sent over to northern France:

I joined the army when I was 17¹/₂ [and] trained to be a tank driver ... About August '44 I went over to France and I started driving a [Firefly] tank then, and I got through and we pulled back to Ypres in Belgium to re-equip ... The war wasn't too good at times, we had two hits on our tank but fortunately they didn't do us any harm, they just hit the back of the tank and ricocheted off. You get a bit shaken up with it, you know. But ... after a while you just carry on driving ... I consider myself lucky that I did come through the war without getting hurt, after seeing some of my comrades getting killed.

The factory may also have been working on some other tank prototypes or designs at the time because Albert Thurling, then a delivery boy working for the local Co-op, remembers bringing food to the canteen at ROF Hayes in 1944 or 45 and seeing some strange new tanks:

We got to see some of the things that were coming out. One thing that stuck in my mind was a tank, but no turret on it or gun, it had an antenna and dish-type aerial on the top instead.

Ronald Teague just after the war

A Sherman Firefly IC in the town square of Putanges in Normandy, 20 August 1944, photographed by Sergeant Gee

ROF HAYES
AFTER THE WAR

The post-war fate of the ROFs was being considered before the war had actually ended, as early as 1943; it was assumed that around half would be retained for military or government use, with others being sold off to private industry or converted into trading estates to encourage new business. ROF Hayes finally closed in November 1946, and it was one of several ordnance factory sites that were retained as storage depots, in the case of Hayes as a Ministry of Supply depot.

In 1950 the site of ROF Hayes was taken over by the Public Record Office as an 'intermediate depository', where records could be held before eventual archiving or disposal. Huge quantities of metal archive racking – a total of about 210 miles – were installed in the former machine sheds. In 1960 shed Y was split into eight sealed bays, separated by full-height asbestos and steel 'firebreak' partitions in order to protect the most sensitive records. The records stored here included those of many government ministries, such as the Ministry of Farming and Fishing, of Defence, of Education and of Transport.

ProLogis Park Heathrow: the major warehousing centre currently being built on the site of the former ordnance factory

Post-war archive racking installed in one of
the former wartime machine sheds

The Imperial War Museum was also allowed to use part of the site. In 1959 the museum
opened a new photographic and film archive here, building an office and a microfilm
and tape storage building in the 1970s.

Ronald Teague – who had visited the factory as a young tank driver in 1944 – came
back to the site in the late 1980s, this time working as a security guard in what was
known as the government Custody Service:

> We used to start work at six o'clock at night and carry on till eight o'clock in the
> morning. One of us would go round every two hours with a clock, clocking where
> you'd been, and it tells you what time you'd been to these different places you had to
> go to, so you couldn't go round and miss anything! There was all sorts of documents
> there. The War Office had documents, the police, civil servants. I worked there about
> two years.

In the 1990s, a strip of land on the west of the site was lost to the new Heathrow Express railway line, which opened in 1998 and runs between Paddington and Heathrow. In 1996, the site was given to the Ministry of Defence for use as an MoD archive, although it continued to store civilian records such as those of the Home Office, Metropolitan Police and Magistrates Courts.

In 2003, ownership and management of the site passed to the ProLogis/TNT consortium following the privatisation – controversial at the time – of parts of the government's records management. The Hayes records were electronically indexed and transferred to a new purpose-built TNT facility in Swadlincote in Derbyshire. The former ROF site is being redeveloped as a warehouse centre, known as ProLogis Park Heathrow, situated in an advantageous position close to Europe's busiest airport.

Demolition in 2005 of one of the
former machine sheds of ROF Hayes

The history of the wartime Royal Ordnance Factories was first told by Ian Hay in his 1949 book *ROF: the story of the Royal Ordnance Factories, 1939–49*. The book does not have much detail specifically about ROF Hayes, although the front cover shows a woman from the factory working on a 25-pounder gun. A more detailed history of the ROFs and the other wartime factories can be found in the official government series *History of the Second World War*, in the volumes entitled *Factories and plant* (by W Hornby, published in 1958) and *British war production* (by M Postan, published in 1952). Mark Hayward's *Sherman Firefly* is an excellent and well-illustrated account of the tank (published by Barbarossa Books in 2001). For more detailed information on the guns

The front cover of the 1949 book *ROF: the story of the Royal Ordnance Factories 1939–48*: the original caption reads '*Machining a 25-pounder at ROF Hayes*'

and other weapons produced at ROF Hayes it is best to start with *World War 2 Fact Files*, a series of illustrated books published by Macdonald and Jane's in the 1970s. *Fortress Britain: working lives and trade unions in World War II* (published by the National Pensioners Convention in 2005) is a superb collection of oral testimony, principally of factory workers. Catherine Kelter's book, *Hayes: a concise history*, has good background information on Hayes during the war (published by Hillingdon Library in 2003).

Much of the information in this book comes from wartime records preserved in The National Archives in Kew. One can easily search under 'Royal Ordnance Factory' and 'ROF' in the electronic catalogue, but the most useful documents are TNA, SUPP 5/1260 ('Historical notes on the ROFs'), TNA, AVIA 46/278 ('Extracts and papers relating to engineering ROFs'), TNA, AVIA 46/309 ('ROF cost of construction, financial statements & data 1935–1943') and TNA, INF 2/44 (file 1–45: photographs). The local studies room at the London Borough of Hillingdon's Central Library in Uxbridge is another useful source of information and it holds the 'Hayes and Harlington ARP incident file', which records wartime bomb strikes. The Imperial War Museum holds several photographs of ROF Hayes (P 1016–1032) and a fascinating 1942 Ministry of Information film, *Work party*, showing women munitions workers at ROF Hayes (COI 947). The film concentrates on the Herrick family and friends at work; they leave ROF Hayes and go home to Mary Herrick's 21st birthday party.

Museum of London Archaeology (MOLA) carried out the architectural recording of the factory in 2005 before its demolition. All the records – drawings, maps, notes, reports, photographs and sound recordings – are held by the Museum of London's London Archaeological Archive and Research Centre (LAARC) under the site code MOD05.

ACKNOWLEDGEMENTS

ProLogis is the world's largest owner, manager and developer of distribution facilities and they redeveloped the former ROF Hayes site in partnership with TNT and the Ministry of Defence. Throughout the planning and construction of the new ProLogis Park Heathrow they have worked hard to reduce the environmental and heritage impact of the project. They paid for a below-ground archaeological survey of the site, they commissioned the architectural recording of the buildings and they generously funded the research and writing of this publication. ProLogis have also carried out extensive environmental and landscape works, including planting new native species of trees to enhance the indigenous local woodland, and even ensuring the careful rehousing of three badger setts to a new home in the woods! Our particular thanks go to Mark Shepherd of ProLogis.

Several Museum of London Archaeology specialists helped with the project, in particular Tony Mackinder. We would also like to thank David Bowsher, Catherine Drew, Jane Dunn, Nick Elsden, Richard Hewett, Isca Howell, Dave Lakin, Dave Mackie, Andrew Westman and Robin Wroe-Brown (all of MOLA) and Annette Day (Museum of London).

The author pulling open one of the 1960s fire-proof doors in building Y

Mary Scully in 2009

We are also grateful to Jane Jarvis, of Fragment Films, who found (in the Imperial War Museum) the fascinating 1942 film *Work party* about ROF Hayes, and who tracked down and interviewed its star, Mary Scully (in 1942 she was 21-year-old Mary Herrick). Jane used this material in the Anglia TV social history series *The way we were*. Episode 9 was called 'The home front' and juxtaposed the old and new footage of Mary Scully to great effect.

Harry Kale was in charge of security at the Hayes site in 2005 and he kindly escorted the Museum of London staff around the site, provided temporary office accommodation and helped in other ways.

Nick Holder would like to thank John McDonnell MP for the invitation to speak at the 2005 Hayes and Harlington Local History Conference, whose theme was 'Memories of the Second World War: the home front in Hayes and Harlington'. Nick first met at this conference several of those who have contributed their recollections of the factory.

Ronald Teague in 2006 at the Ardennen Poteau '44 Museum, Belgium

A final round of thanks to all those who generously contributed their memories of ROF Hayes and the many family members who helped us out (in particular June Beak, Rebecca Howes and Ron Teague). We would also like to pay tribute to the numerous other men and women who worked at the factory during the war.

Plan of the World War II
Royal Ordnance Factory
at Hayes

N

Stockley Road

KEY

Buildings with wartime letter codes:

A	main machine shed
B	first-aid post?
C	canteen and kitchen
D	surgery
E & F	storage sheds
G–J	garages
K	workshop
L & N	security
O	administration
P	main gate security
Q	storage shed
R	oil store
T	plant
U	boiler house
V	central stores
W	steel pool
Y	main machine shed

Other buildings:

1–11	air-raid shelters
12–15	pillboxes (15 is to north-east of factory)
16–18	observation posts
19	west gate
20	railway gate
21	rail shed
22	weighbridge
23	loading ramp
24–25	'Tarran' huts
26–27	water tanks
28	pond

21

W
steel po

19